SELECTED WORKS

for

CELLO & PIANO

composed by

HELEN C. CRANE

ACCOMPANIMENT EDITION
cello edition sold separately

FULL SCORE

Bernard R. Crane
Editor

ISBN 978-1-7358882-5-5
BISAC: MUS037130
LOC Classification: M6 – 175.5

all pieces copyrighted under the title Collected Chamber Works of Helen C. Crane - Book I
©2020 Bernard R. Crane
ASCAP

Helen C. Crane in her mid 20's (c. 1890)
enhanced photograph of Helen C. Crane as pictured in the publication
"The Music Monitor" July. 1919 – Vol. VIII, No. 10

THE COMPOSER

Helen Cornelia Crane was born September 5, 1868, just a few short years after the end of the Civil War to Col. Alexander Baxter Crane, a native of Massachusetts and his young wife, Laura Cornelia Mitchell, a native of South Carolina. Col. Alexander Crane, a legal studies graduate of Amherst College was commissioned an officer on the side of the North and his young wife was daughter of the John Wroughton Mitchell family of South Carolina who for generations had lived in that part of the country. Certainly their relatives and acquaintances embraced both sides of the chasm that divided the nation. To this young couple was born Helen Cornelia, and along with four sisters and one brother. Their earliest home was St. Mark's Place in New York's lower east side. Eventually Col. Crane's law career led to a flourishing Wall Street legal practice and they purchased property and built their permanent home in Scarsdale, NY.

She must have exhibited artistic talent at a young age since by her late teens she was embarked on studies in music in one of the most enviable of locations...Europe. She studied at the then "Klindworth-Scharwenka" Conservatory in Berlin. These studies culminated in her choice of composition as her major musical endeavor and she studied three years with noted composer and conservatory director Philipp Scharwenka. She was soon winning competitions and gaining much warranted recognition. German publishing houses recognized her work and she saw the publication of numerous of her pieces. Maintaining a regular home in Germany over the next couple of decades, she made several cross-Atlantic voyages for the sake of concertizing and teaching; one such trip in 1904 was for the purpose of hearing the Berlin Philharmonic perform her tone poem, *The Last Tournament* at the "world's fair" the *St. Louis Exposition* that year. She continued her intercontinental career until the guns of World War I made it decidedly unsafe to continue.

At this time she returned to the her family home in Scarsdale, NY a place they affectionately nicknamed "Holmhurst" and here she remained for the most part; barring a few excursions & trip to Kaprun, Austria, where she traveled one last time "for the purpose of her health". Ultimately she passed away in November, 1930 in Scarsdale, NY and was laid to rest in the cemetery of St. James Episcopal Church alongside her parents. She left behind her hand-written manuscripts in the care of her remaining siblings. Her youngest sister, Laura Vernon Crane Burgess ultimately donated this valuable trust to the New York Public Library, where the collection has been housed since the 1940's. Most of these pieces are there in their original manuscript form, showing the evolution of Ms. Crane's calligraphy and the blossoming of musical art. Among these works are over eighty works for the piano, several chamber works, orchestral tone poems such as *The Last Tournament*: her *Evangeline Overture, Cassandra* for female voice and orchestra, her *Serenade* for orchestra, two symphonies, *Psalm 42* for orchestra and chorus along with a multitude of song settings of various poets and pieces for organ. She was well noted in her day, garnering a spot in *Baker's Dictionary of Musicians* and was duly noted in various music histories of the time. But time is not always kind in its passing. Sometimes lives are dwarfed by events that overtake them in the memories of future generations. Bach was forgotten until Mendelssohn revived the memory of his music. And so it has been with Helen C. Crane. With this edition of her chamber works hopefully our quiet sister speaks again. Let today's performers and today's listener be the judge. As a composer and as a music theorist, I do believe she warrants serious consideration. She stands as an integral part of the flowing forth of what is a truly "American" music, her life spanning that period of time between the Civil War and the "Great Depression", a time period known as the "Belle Époque", "the gilded age", a time shaken, rocked and irretrievably lost to an even greater war, World War I. Ms. Crane occupies a unique spot between late romanticism and the subsequent quest for new expression in music, enjoining her efforts to those of others, pushing the limits of tonality and yet retaining the memorable communication of which music is most capable.

Bernard Crane
Jan. 17, 2019

DAYS OF DISCOVERY

Just a few minutes of spare time and a bit of curiosity is all that it took to launch myself on a quest that has now encompassed the last two years. Thanks to the wonders of the digital age more and more information is accumulated in smaller and smaller formats, occupying less and less space. Where once the entire floor of an office building was necessary to house one computer, now an entire library of reading material can be stored on a device not much larger than a little finger. One of the results of this every burgeoning ability to collect, store, and share materials is a unique collective enterprise known as International Music Score Library Project or IMSLP, present online at www.imslp.org . With the cooperation of individuals, schools and universities, through the pooling of resources we have reached a point where a significant portion of published music that is no longer copyright, is now available. In light of this rich source which I have used many times in the past, and being a composer myself, with degrees from Eastman and the San Francisco Conservatory, I was curious if there were any other CRANE's listed on IMSLP website. I did find five: Adam Crane, a gentleman who seems to have been more of a performer or teacher than a composer: his one page inclusion was "NiffTShift" some sort of performance method for shifting positions on a stringed instrument. Perhaps technically helpful, but artistically, not much. Frederick L. Crane: in some spots labeled "Fred L. Crane" - "After The Ball - a romance": having no relation to the old standard "gay nineties" tune; a brief piano piece, showy but with little integrity in the melodic line, harmony, in essence - blasé; J. W. Crane "2 Romances Sans Paroles": published in 1877 by Hartmann in Paris, very much "à la Mendelsohn or J. Burgmüller"; again, nice but not "earth-shaking". There was an entry for Lucy Crane, who apparently was sister of the noted illustrator Walter Crane, - her contribution is entitled "Baby's Opera"; (my thought on seeing the title, one might have difficulty holding the attention of either the cast, the audience or both.) Upon a closer look I see that it is a collection of nursery rhymes put to melody, which melodies she ascribed to "great masters of the past", so she is in fact the editor of the collection accompanied by artistic images of her brother, the noted illustrator. That leaves us with one remaining composer: Helen C. Crane and the "one" oeuvre that is listed here: her "Piano Trio in E Major, op.20". One piece, three movements, about 60 printed pages total, published in Germany by Gustav Vetter in 1907. I quickly ran off a copy, and waited anxiously for some spare time to run through it.

Eventually the opportunity came, one hour before a choral rehearsal which I was directing. When I began playing through the music I was actually amazed: it was quite bold, rather forward thinking; perhaps post-Brahms-ian, as one would hope, adventurous in its interrelation of keys, soaring melodies wonderful orchestration with each part very much in keeping with the technical parameters of each instrument. It seemed to be loaded with nuance, deeper meaning and ideas that warranted further study and repeated listening. There was certainly nothing wrong with any of the facets of the work, it showed great attention to detail, correct in all musical parameters on its face. I enjoyed the piece, beginning to end.

Opus 20 implied there had to be at least 19 other pieces or groupings of various sizes and instrumentation perhaps, but where were they? Were they ever published? What became of them? My mind was abuzz with curiosity and in the ensuing days I began some intensive exploration, running google searches and more, and it was not long before I came across an interesting discovery: in doing a search for "Helen C. Crane composer" I was ushered to a "url" which detailed a bequest from a New York City family to the city's library of all their important documents. This collection according to what I was able to ascertain was the Alexander Crane family's personal correspondence and spanned a period of more than a century, from the early 1800's to about 1940. Apparently Alexander was a personage of some note in New York City, enough so to warrant gathering together all of his correspondence in the NY Public Library. Closer examination showed that he was a Wall Street lawyer, a commissioned officer in the Civil War, and there was some sort of diplomatic connections in Italy,...why would this search for Helen Crane have brought me here?

Scanning through the contents of the collection which included a listing of family members, I came across Helen Cornelia Crane. Come to find out Helen C. Crane was Alexander's daughter and gradually the pieces began to fall into place. Helen's materials were not located with this larger collection at the main library. Rather her materials were housed at the NYPL "Cullman Center" Library for the Performing Arts at 40 Lincoln Center Plaza. When I checked this particular library's Helen C. Crane Collection listing, I was shocked! It was all there*; everything, either in its original manuscript form or both manuscript and published form along with ephemera concerning performances, playbills, requests from the Library of Congress for copies of awarded pieces, notes concerning her publishing agreements and records of payment, etc. a veritable mother-lode of material.

The only exception being her "Elegy for Cello" op. 57 for which she was awarded a prize in 1918. The Library of Congress subsequently requested a copy for their records (1944). Helen, having passed away in 1930, her sister, Caroline Crane Marsh obliged the Library of Congress, gifting them with what would seem to have been the only copy of the work. Hence, that work is no longer in the NYPL collection.

She was born in 1868 the second child with four sisters and a brother. She must have been very talented and showed a keen interest in the study of music. She ended up a student of Xaver Scharwenka, a noted Polish pianist and composer, who was performing and teaching from NYC at that time. Xaver's brother, Philip was also a musician, a pianist, composer, and educator and was director of the Klindworth-Scharwenka Conservatory in Berlin, Germany. I can only surmise that having worked with Ms. Crane, Scharwenka, became aware of her gifts and abilities and potential. With a brother heading up a conservatory in Europe, perhaps that would be the logical continuation of her studies, at this Berlin Conservatory with his brother as her composition teacher.

According to the NYPL Performance Library division whose listings I was able to find online, there were somewhere in the vicinity of 4 cu. ft. of original and published manuscripts of Helen's writings. The list included notations as to the nature of its contents, the various opus numbers, methods of copy, pen, pencil or published. It looked as though everything was there, however the breadth of her output was a bit larger than 20: there are 74 numbered works. ...op. 74 being her last. Included in her output were two symphonies with sketches for a 3rd, several symphonic tone-poems, well over 200 works for piano, choral works, songs for solo voice, sonatas for violin, cello, a larger work for orchestra and chorus. It was amazing.

I soon made my way to NYC to get a first hand look at this Collection that was locked away in the archives and only available by appointment. It was amazing to see the extent of the collection neatly housed in seventeen archival boxes. The documents were in pristine condition, bearing no impression they had been even touched since the day the were donated. The Library made no claims to copyright and certainly the pieces were past statutory protection (all except op.74 composed before 1923). They could not let the documents be photocopied but there was no prohibition on available-light images taken with a camera or cellphone. Over the next year with three successive visits to NY I came away with some 3,440 images of Helen's own manuscripts.

In sharing this music with others, people have asked the obvious question: "with the same last name, are you related to her?" Well, it is an interesting question: Ellery Bicknell Crane in his 2 - volume set "The Cranes of Massachusetts" (pub. 1900) does a masterful job of tracing our family's ancestry back to the mid 17th century and to the immigration of a handful of Cranes who came to the New World. There were two brothers, Henry & Benjamin, and their father John Crane, who landed in Boston, and described themselves as being of "Muddy Brook" (generally the area around today's Boston University). The boys eventually moved once again to the Wethersfield colony on the Connecticut River. Another "Henry" Crane was located in the area of Milton, MA. He himself had a son and a grandson also named Benjamin, as if there might be some naming after, an uncle of ancestor, but there is at this time, no conclusive evidence.

Alexander Crane is descended from the Henry Crane of Milton, MA, I am descended from Benjamin Crane of Connecticut, son of John Crane, Muddy Brook or Boston, MA. If there is a connection it would be father of John and that would make Helen & myself eighth cousins, four times removed. But that matters little. The music is what matters and it is here and available, no longer sequestered away on a dusty library shelf. And the music speaks for itself.

            Bernard Crane
           arranger & editor   *January, 2019*

SELECTED WORKS *for* CELLO & PIANO

composed by

HELEN C. CRANE

TABLE OF CONTENTS

SCORE

I	Idyll for Cello & Piano No.1	p. 1
	from Six Idylls for Cello op.51	
II	Idyll for Cello & Piano No.2	p. 5
	from Six Idylls for Cello op.51	
III	Idyll for Cello & Piano No. 3	p. 8
	from Six Idylls for Cello op.51	
IV	Idyll for Cello & Piano No. 4	p.13
	from Six Idylls for Cello op.51	
V	Idyll for Cello & Piano No. 5	p.16
	from Six Idylls for Cello op.51	
VI	Idyll for Cello & Piano No. 6	p.19
	from Six Idylls for Cello op.51	
VII	Morgenständchen *(Morning Serenade)* for Cello & Piano Op.17	p.23

Idyll
for Cello & Piano

No.1

Helen C. Crane
Op. 51 no. 1

© 2020 Bernard R. Crane
all rights reserved

Helen C. Crane — Idyll — Op.51 no. 1

Idyll
for Cello & Piano
No. 2

Helen C. Crane
Op. 51 no.2

©2020 Bernard R. Crane
all rights reserved

Helen C. Crane # Idyll # Op. 51 no.2

Idyll
for Cello & Piano

No. 3

Helen C. Crane
Op. 51 no. 3

© 2020 Bernard R. Crane
all rights reserved

Idyll

Idyll
for Cello & Piano
No. 4

Helen C. Crane
Op. 51 no. 4

©2019 Bernard R. Crane
all rights reserved

Idyll

Helen C. Crane — Idyll — Op.51 no. 1

Idyll
for Cello & Piano
No. 5

Helen C. Crane
Op. 51 no. 5

Idyll

18   Helen C. Crane   Op. 51 no. 5

Idyll
for Cello & Piano
No. 6

Helen C. Crane
Op. 51 no. 6

©2020 Bernard R. Crane
all rights reserved

Helen C. Crane — Idyll — Op.51 no. 6

Morgenständchen
Morning Serenade

Helen C. Crane
Op. 16

© 2020 Bernard R. Crane
all rights reserved

Helen C Crane — Morgenstandchen — op.16

Helen C Crane — Morgenstandchen — op.16

Helen C Crane — Morgenstandchen — op.16

Helen C Crane — Morgenstandchen — op.16

Helen C Crane — Morgenstandchen — op.16

Helen C Crane — Morgenstandchen — op.16

www.ingramcontent.com/pod-product-compliance
Lightning Source LLC
LaVergne TN
LVHW061344060426
835512LV00016B/2660